THE FOUR FUNDAMENTAL ASPECTS OF LOVE

*Based on
"The Transcripts of Mary Magdalene"*

CHERYL JACKSON

The Four Fundamental Aspects of Love
Based on "The Transcripts of Mary Magdalene"

Copyright © 2020, Cheryl Jackson

The views expressed by the author in reference to specific people in their book represent entirely their own individual opinions and are not in any way reflective of the views of Capucia, LLC. We assume no responsibility for errors, omissions, or contradictory interpretation of the subject matter herein.

Capucia, LLC does not warrant the performance, effectiveness, or applicability of any websites listed in or linked to this publication. The purchaser or reader of this publication assumes responsibility for the use of these materials and information. Capucia, LLC shall in no event be held liable to any party for any direct, indirect, punitive, special, incidental, or any other consequential damages arising directly or indirectly from any use of this material. Techniques and processes given in this book are not to be used in place of medical or other professional advice.

No part of this book may be reproduced or transmitted in any form, or by any means, electronic or mechanical, including photography, recording, or in any information storage or retrieval system without written permission from the author or publisher, except in the case of brief quotations embodied in articles and reviews.

Capucia
PUBLISHING

Published by:
Capucia, LLC
211 Pauline Drive #513
York, PA 17402
www.capuciapublishing.com

Paperback ISBN: 978-1-954920-21-7
Hardback ISBN: 978-1-945252-89-1
eBook ISBN: 978-1-945252-88-4
Library of Congress Control Number: 2020912906

Cover Design: Ranilo Cabo
Layout: Ranilo Cabo
Editor and Proofreader: Gwen Hoffnagle
Book Midwife: Carrie Jareed

Printed in the United States of America

Prologue

When Judy Satori first released the "Transcripts of Mary Magdalene" programs, I was curious. Many others claim to channel Mary Magdalene, but having already done some of Judy's transmissions, meditations and teachings, she seemed more authentic. With her personal calling from Mary Magdalene to travel to La Sainte Baume, Provence, France, to record Mary's lectures and channelings for the first program, I was very impressed.

When she explained that this is the way Jesus and Mary Magdalene taught, I was totally hooked. I listened to all of the meditations, transmissions and channelings at least three times as suggested.

At the end of my first round of listening to the first "Journey to Amenti," I received the symbol of four spirals along with a bracelet on each wrist of seven strands of copper-colored light with sacred symbols from the Lords of Amenti. Not knowing what it all meant, I continued with Judy's second and third programs of Mary Magdalene transcripts. Years passed by and they remained curiosities in my life.

When a friend of mine asked me what I really wanted to do with all of my New Age teachings, out of my mouth popped, "I want to write a book." Within days I received the compositions "Beautiful Petal" and "The Invitation." Others soon followed so I asked my angels and guides to organize the compositions along the structure of the Tarot card system.

That was when the symbol of the four spirals came blazing back into my mind. I decided to listen one more time to the "Journey to Amenti" because of the gifts I had received. "The Story" section in *The Four Fundamental Aspects of Love* is a fictionalized account, based on my vision of this meditation that also provides context for the compositions. It does not include the powerful energy transmissions in multidimensional, spiritual languages that Judy channeled during the meditations. Therefore I have asked Spirit to bless the reader with any needed healing energies as they experience each page of the book.

For those new to Tarot, the cards are organized into Major and Minor Arcana. The Major Arcana are cards numbered zero to twenty-one and represent life's journey from birth to death. The Minor Arcana has four suits of fourteen cards each that represent the more daily aspects of life – physical, mental, emotional and spiritual. They are used to find hidden meanings and guidance. The book is divided into these sections as well.

The purpose of the compositions is to provide a gentle, easy to use and practical tool to practice making the Four Fundamental Aspects of Love a part of your everyday living. I suggest reading all of the compositions through once. When you find some that speak to you, reread them on a regular basis. There are many paths that lead to love. This book is about giving you loving guidance to assist you in finding your own unique path to love.

If you want to listen to the same impactful meditations from "The Transcripts of Mary Magdalene – The Fundamental Aspects of Love," as I did, you can visit www.AscensionLibrary.com for all of Judy's Ascension acceleration programs. Then move on to the second and third Mary Magdalene programs. You will be glad you did.

Judy Satori is an Activator of Human Potential who speaks multidimensional, spiritual languages of new creation. These languages are of God, Source, and love. Her work is to upgrade and activate more of our human DNA genetic code as part of a divinely orchestrated plan for Earth and her people.

The Fundamental Aspects of Love

This is a set of teachings and energy transmissions received by Judy Satori from Mary Magdalene and other higher dimensional spiritual beings. "The Transcripts of Mary Magdalene" is a truly remarkable nine-part, 14-MP3 audio program that balances the four fundamental aspects of love within the heart and opens you to be able to give and receive more love in your life.

Being Love: Gateway to Joy

This second part of the Mary Magdalene program consolidates and strengthens the fourth of the fundamental aspects of love, *Loving Being-ness*. This is your ability to just *be* and resonate with the love vibration. This program energetically instills the love vibration into every cell of your body. This enhances your ability to give and receive love; supports the physical, emotional and deep healing of the soul; and helps you resonate with and bring *joy* into your life.

Joy Is Love Expressed

Judy is completing a three-year journey with Mary Magdalene. "Joy is Love Expressed" is the final chapter of the "Transcripts of Mary Magdalene," a set of teachings about *love*. Mary's teachings began with the fundamental aspects of love and balancing four aspects of love within the heart, and progressed to being love… actually anchoring a higher energy of love within the cells of the body.

Dearly Beloved Divine Oneness, who has given me life,

If it is in my highest good and the highest good for all life everywhere, please help me learn to open my heart, raise my awareness to balance my life with all life and integrate you into my life in all seven directions — North, South, East, West, Above, Below and Within - gracefully. Thank you and Amen.

Contents

Beautiful Petal 1
The Story 3
The Invitation 27

The Journey – Major life transitions 29
   Zero: Beginnings 30
   One: Awareness 31
   Two: Intuition 32
   Three: Fertility 33
   Four: Authority 34
   Five: Tradition 35
   Six: Union 36
   Seven: Victory 37

Eight: Strength ... 38
Nine: Introspection ... 39
Ten: Destiny ... 40
Eleven: Justice ... 41
Twelve: Release ... 42
Thirteen: Transition ... 43
Fourteen: Balance ... 44
Fifteen: Redemption ... 45
Sixteen: Upheaval ... 46
Seventeen: Renewal ... 47
Eighteen: Illusion ... 48
Nineteen: Success ... 49
Twenty: Rebirth ... 50
Twenty-One: Integration ... 51

Loving Wisdom – Mental, Intellect, Air Element ... 53

One: Clarity ... 54
Two: Indecision ... 55
Three: Separation ... 56
Four: Recuperation ... 57
Five: Betrayal ... 58
Six: Passage ... 59

SEVEN: DECEPTION	60
EIGHT: IMPRISONMENT	61
NINE: DEPRESSION	62
TEN: DEFEAT	63
ELEVEN: CURIOUS	64
TWELVE: OPINIONATED	65
THIRTEEN: PERCEPTIVE	66
FOURTEEN: INTELLECTUAL	67

LOVING KINDNESS – EMOTIONS, RELATIONSHIPS, WATER ELEMENT   69

ONE: LOVE	70
TWO: RELATIONSHIPS	71
THREE: CELEBRATION	72
FOUR: CONTEMPLATION	73
FIVE: DESPAIR	74
SIX: NOSTALGIA	75
SEVEN: CHOICES	76
EIGHT: DISAPPOINTMENT	77
NINE: SATISFACTION	78
TEN: HARMONY	79
ELEVEN: SYNCHRONICITY	80
TWELVE: CHARM	81

THIRTEEN: CALM   82
FOURTEEN: COUNSELOR   83

LOVING STRENGTH– PASSIONS, ACTION, FIRE ELEMENT   85
ONE: POTENTIAL   86
TWO: DISCOVERY   87
THREE: EXPANSION   88
FOUR: HOMECOMING   89
FIVE: CONFLICT   90
SIX: CONFIDENCE   91
SEVEN: PERSEVERANCE   92
EIGHT: ACCELERATION   93
NINE: PERSISTENCE   94
TEN: RESPONSIBILITY   95
ELEVEN: ENTHUSIASM   96
TWELVE: IMPULSIVENESS   97
THIRTEEN: VIBRANCY   98
FOURTEEN: VISION   99

LOVING BEING-NESS – MATERIAL,
PHYSICAL, EARTH ELEMENT … 101
   ONE: PROSPERITY … 102
   TWO: ADAPTABILITY … 103
   THREE: COLLABORATION … 104
   FOUR: STABILITY … 105
   FIVE: ISOLATION … 106
   SIX: GENEROSITY … 107
   SEVEN: REWARD … 108
   EIGHT: EDUCATION … 109
   NINE: DISCIPLINE … 110
   TEN: ACCOMPLISHMENT … 111
   ELEVEN: MANIFESTATION … 112
   TWELVE: METHODICAL … 113
   THIRTEEN: PRACTICAL … 114
   FOURTEEN: ABUNDANCE … 115

ABOUT THIS BOOK … 117
ABOUT THE AUTHOR … 119
ACKNOWLEDGMENTS … 121

Beautiful Petal

*Beautiful petal of God's own hue
Delighting Creator with all you do
To spread the light and love and joy
As each of its purposes is deployed.*

*Beautiful petal that seeks the sun,
You move unerringly towards the love
That lies awake to hear your call
Answering your every thought, enthralled.*

*Beautiful petal, the color of God,
Same as the flowers and trees.
Beautiful in our differences
As are all the fish in the seas.*

*Beautiful petal, rise and dance.
The wind lifts your love so true
To the sun and the stars above and beyond
To kiss the star-flung hues.*

The Story

This is a short story of how the symbol of the four spirals appeared during a trip to Amenti and became a symbol of the four fundamental aspects of love – Loving Wisdom, Loving Kindness, Loving Strength and Loving Being-ness.

As I looked out my window, I thought to myself, "What a glorious day!" After a few minutes of contemplating the sunny view, I glanced around my home and decided that whatever I had planned to do that day had to wait. I needed to get out there and inhale that sunshine. Grabbing my phone on my way to the door, I ran out and practically skipped down the sidewalk.

Glorious day, indeed! It even smelled like a glorious day! Birds singing. Sunshine on my face with puffy white clouds to keep me company. Chuckling, I asked myself, "How could it get any better than this?"

Then I remembered a small neighborhood park down the way that the city was in the process of upgrading with new playground equipment and landscaping. Curious about the project, I sauntered through the entryway. The city had also added a new dog park, a walking trail and a beautiful round, stone moon gate.

Up the new steps and through the gate opening I could see a tranquil field with trees. A gentle breeze ruffled their leaves and, at the same time, beckoned me to enter the peace-filled space. Intrigued by the possibilities, I walked through the gate and onto the walkway of that beautiful field.

Under a giant elm tree stood a tall, graceful being radiating white light. Her smile was warm and inviting. She turned to me and said, "You have been called and you have answered. Welcome." Enchanted by her smile, I joined her and took her outstretched hand.

"I want you to join me on a journey. A journey of exploration to the place of inner earth called Amenti, which resides within Agartha. When the ancient Lemurian civilization disintegrated in the sinking of her vast landmass in the Pacific, some of the survivors went underground to a place that came to be known as Agartha. They were able to because, at that time, they still resonated with very high-frequency energy and they could exist within the inner earth kingdoms, which vibrate much faster than the surface of the Earth. For a long time they could come and go with ease, but as the surface of the Earth became denser and the consciousness of the people descended vibrationally, the entranceways to Agartha were sealed off and only those with pure heart and expanded vibrational energies could actually gain access. Although no one actually lives in Amenti, it is the place of the seven lords and holds the pulse rhythms of the Earth. Amenti is the source of all knowledge and truth for this planet.

"Now please understand that to be successful on this journey, you must merge consciousness, peace, love and oneness with all life within your heart. Your heart must be pure to be admitted. We will be passing through seven gates, each relating to the seven bodies of man. At each one you will be challenged, but if you stay focused on truth, you will move forward. If you don't, you will be sent back to try again. This is a process of initiation, and to receive this knowledge you must also demonstrate worthiness and readiness for this higher instruction. Will you come?"

Looking deeply into her eyes, I nodded, establishing mutual trust.

"Before we go, close your eyes and imagine a great golden-white light coming from above your head, from the Heart of Creation, passing through your non-dominant side and reaching down to the Heart of the Earth. Now imagine a grounding silver-green light coming up from the Heart of the Earth, passing through your dominant side and reaching to the Heart of Creation. They meet and mix in your body's heart area. The flow and ebb of that light helps you become aware of your breath, your heartbeat, and your mind as all three are now connected. Allow your mind to drift out to all life around us. To the grass and trees. To the birds and clouds. Connect now with the God Mind, joining with The Oneness of the All. Do you feel the expansion? Yes? Open your eyes. We are now ready to proceed."

She explained that we would be traveling through a portal in time and space – an interdimensional gateway to the inner earth kingdoms. She turned away, and with a wave of her arm, opened what looked like a whirlpool of light. From deep inside the center came a faint hum and pulse rhythm. She instructed me to quietly match my heartbeat to the pulses, becoming one with Earth. After speaking certain words to give us safe passage through the portal, she led us through and we started to descend.

The first gate was guarded by a scorpion and has to do with the physical body. It was explained to me that my physical self is only a reflection of my consciousness manifested into form. As my consciousness rises into the higher dimensions, so my body reflects these changes. It is the way of this journey. My guide advised me to remain calm; to hold on to my energy of peace, love and oneness. The scorpion guardian eyed us warily but assessed us to be worthy, allowing us to pass. I bowed to its light and thanked it for its service to the light. As we walked through the gate, I could feel my body being alchemically altered to adjust to the higher dimensional energies of inner earth.

I then noticed a bright light ahead of us.

My guide told me that this is the Light of Hope. She told me that it always burns for this planet and is never unattended. The brightest light, the greatest hope, is for the day that the surface-dwellers and those of the inner kingdoms may once more be together as one people upon the Earth. "Hope," she said, "is activated conviction. Despair never gets the last word."

We then walked on to the second gate, adorned with a regal, golden lioness statue. This gate relates to the emotional body of man. I gazed into the eyes of the lioness and saw the reflected truth of myself. I could hear, in my mind, the statue speak of the courage and strength that lies in my ability to be peace, love and one with all life; to always remember to defend my truth as a lioness defends her cubs. She advised me to always search inside for the answers to life. She reminded me of how important it is to release sabotaging, self-defeating emotions and to step fully into the higher-dimensional consciousness of peace, love and unity. I bowed to her light and thanked her for sharing her wisdom. The lioness graciously allowed us to pass through her Gate of Hope.

As we moved forward, my guide spoke more magical words as the passage narrowed and steeply descended. We were soon enveloped by soft, green mist. Ahead of us were the three guardians for the third gate, which relates to the mental body and the thoughts that create all of reality. The Three Graces asked me to look deeply into the three aspects of my mind.

The first Grace explained that the first aspect, the lower mind, thinks in terms of irritation and blame, and is self-focused. She advised me to see it as an illusion, as it is not real. It keeps me from the light. If I was now ready to rise above these thought forms, I was to ask inside my heart that this be so. She then spoke the magical words to secure this for me.

The second Grace asked me to connect with the higher mind of my soul and spirit that is the place of True Grace. She requested that I surrender to the power of God and the power of Love. In so doing, one is forever free, forever whole, and can stand in the truth of one's own light, which is the light of God.

The third Grace came bearing a silver-white orb of stone. She instructed me to hold it to the middle of my forehead, also known as my third eye. As I did so, I gained entrance to the causal plane of mental thought, the place of abstract thought that is connected to all thought and the mind of God. I felt my human mind expand to touch a loving cosmic mind and felt our connection to all life. I returned the orb of stone to the third Grace when the connection concluded. I had been deemed worthy by the three guardians so we were allowed to pass through the

Gate of the Mind and be free of its control and illusion. I bowed to their light in gratitude for the lessons learned.

The steps were ever steeper now as we approached the fourth gate, the gate of the Buddha. Passing through this gate grants the mantel of spiritual wisdom, power and peace. It was guarded by the powerful and enlightened spirits known as Devas. My guide explained that these are the strong, protective nature spirits of inner earth and are always here for us. They work together to nurture and protect the Earth, their mother. Now they would work together and protect us. She said to speak to them in the mind and they would answer. We asked them for safe passage and the barriers fell. We bowed to their light and in gratitude for all they do. We continued on.

The fifth gate was the Gate of Unity. It is of connection with all that is, of oneness and of coming home. There is no guardian except for the voice of my inner self. My guide explained that I was stepping into the clarity of higher dimensional truth where all are created by the mind. There is no place for anger, dispute or blame of self or others. Only truth, oneness, peace and love may dwell here. I maintained my highest thoughts and my soul allowed me to pass through into the realm of spirit and the true home of my spiritual interdimensional self.

Ahead there was a bright light and open space. We entered a crystalline cavern of light filled with many tall, beautiful light beings who resembled my guide. They smiled and seemed to be waiting for us.

My guide explained, "These are the beings of Lemuria, of Mu, who have lived for a long time within the inner earth, known as Agartha. There are many pathways and passages between their kingdoms and between their different cities. Although Amenti is within Agartha, they do not live inside Amenti. Nobody does except the seven lords who always reside there. These beings of Mu who went within the inner earth also guard this place. And now they welcome you back because you are part of them and they are part of you and you have been here before. But only for a time. You have not stayed because you have decided to incarnate on the surface of the Earth so that you may do more to change and bring the light to the surface-dwellers. And so they welcome you with their hearts. They welcome you with their love and they walk with us as we journey to Amenti."

Their leader stepped out of the group. He was the

leader of all the inner earth kingdoms and had come from Telos to greet us. He said, "So you have come home to the heart of our mother, the Earth. You have come here to this place that is our home, but we are here to take you to Amenti, for Amenti is the place of all becoming and beginnings. Amenti is the place where the pulse rhythms of the Earth are kept and is the place of regenesis of new life for you as it is for all the Earth. This is the place of the sixth gate, the Gate of Divine Love and Oneness with all life; the Gate of Infinite Joy, Infinite Peace; of trust and surrender. Amenti is where you will find what it is you seek. We will escort and assist you as far as the next gate."

In order to pass through the sixth gate, I had to feel ready to trust in eternal love and the protection of the universe to always guide me along the path of the heart. I was ready to trust in God and in my deepest desires as reflections of the truth of my soul. My thoughts were of the highest, and so we continued on through the sixth gate.

My guide and our escorts assisted with my attunement to the seventh gate, for it takes place through both the physical heart and the heart chakras. After I opened my heart to these energies in deep love, peace and communion with all, I received prolonged, deep toning to adjust to the correct frequency. We reclined there until the process was complete, and rested for some time afterwards.

After bowing to their light and thanking our hosts, we continued towards the seventh gate, the passage to Amenti. The passageway was filled with light – brilliant rose-pink suffused with white, suffused with gold, suffused with magenta. The scent of roses and jasmine filled the air.

It was explained to me that the seventh gate is an amplification of a frequency that would attune me to its vibration. The only way through this gateway is with love suffused into joy, a blending of the energies of peace, love and oneness. Then one sends that joy out like a mighty beacon of light, from the mind like a mighty river flowing out, for only joy will open the gate to this place called Amenti.

Walking through the gate, we entered a beautiful garden – a garden more beautiful than any garden I had ever seen. The colors were brilliant and diffuse. There were large, sparkling clusters of crystals of every hue bursting towards the sky. Resident animals, large and small, watched us in confident curiosity. I heard the sound of water from a small bubbling stream running through the beauty of the garden. I was told that these were the waters of new creation for me. I walked down to the stream and scooped up some water in my hands and drank deeply. We continued walking, reveling in the beautiful song of the brightly colored birds, the intoxicating fragrance of the flowers, the whispers of the stately trees and the gentle rustling of the flowering bushes that adorned the path.

Most of all I noticed the stillness and the peace of this place. My guide told me to take the peace and stillness into my being so I might always rely on it. Whenever I needed to create the energies of peace, I could reconnect to the peace that is in Amenti and fashion it for myself, just by connecting with it through my heart and creating the peace within my mind.

As we walked through this garden, music began to play. I was told that this music was the music of my heart and the music of my soul. It was playing a special tune just for me. I stopped to listen and was transfixed by the intricate melodies and deep undertones.

Ahead of us glowed a beautiful golden pavilion. It seemed suspended above the waters of a serene lake that the little stream flowed into. This was the place where we were headed and where we were going to meet some very special beings, she told me. It was time to go and stand before the lords.

At my slight hesitation she said, "You know that you now possess all knowledge and wisdom. When they refuse you entrance, remember the secret words of power that I taught you as we walked in the garden. If your words are of the highest truth and your heart is full of love, the door will open and you will be called into the chamber. You will break the grasp of darkness that binds you to this planet by uncovering the secrets and wisdom of old. You will be forever free to explore all possible futures and join the oneness of all creation that is of God.

"My love, go stand before the Lords and ask to see all possible futures of your soul and hear your reason for being, not only here in Amenti, but on this planet at this time. Hear what it means for you to have won the right to be and to become."

At the entrance to the pavilion we went inside, but when I looked around I was unexpectedly alone. I approached the chamber door and was refused entrance. I spoke the words of power I had learned. When the door swung open, I was called and I entered their chamber of light.

There were lighted sconces along the walls. The room

was circular and filled with light. In front of me was a table fitted into the curvature. On one side of the table, facing me, were sitting seven beings of light, The Seven Lords of Amenti.

"Child of Light," they said to me, "it is time and you are ready. You are welcome here and so we have arrived."

The being in the middle stood. He raised his hand and he blessed me. He spoke to my soul but I heard it through my mind.

"Welcome. I bid you welcome here to this place. We are here together as one. You are to be given the wisdom of the ages. You are to be given the knowledge. You are to be infused with love to be of light. You have discovered the secrets of secrets. You have discovered the way to the God Mind. You have discovered that the way is within the heart and within the mind. When the mind is co-joined with the heart and co-joined with love, which expresses as joy, the way to Amenti is found. And so, too, the way for new life for you and for all the people of the Earth. They can pass through this passage. So we welcome you.

"As I stand, I send a wave of vibration into your

heart. This wave of vibration is to activate the loving nature within you to its highest expression of soul. But this is only possible when the four fundamental aspects of love are balanced within you – Loving Wisdom, Loving Kindness, Loving Strength and Loving Beingness. For this is your work. This is your purpose – to balance the love nature and then you will be free. You will be free of your Earthly lives and free of your Earthly nature. You will rise above all that is of hardship and all that is of pain.

"You will create as the god that you are. Look up to the table now and speak to the Lords and tell them your desires of the heart, for they will listen to you."

As I stood before the Seven Lords of Amenti, I asked my questions and they solemnly answered. I told them of the desires of my heart and they listened. Then each one of the Lords spoke to me of an energy gift they were bestowing on me. Each was received with deep gratitude and everlasting love.

The being in the middle then stated, "Now that you have made it fully to Amenti, it is easy to come here again. When you come here, your physical body, your emotions, your mind, will be recalibrated and be made anew. And you will see the changes occurring within the cells, within the physical appearance, within the energy that you have, within your vitality, within your love nature, within your passion and your purpose. And as you are, so will you attract. As you are, so will you pull into your reality. You will radiate love and light out into the world. Walk a path of service with love and grace, dignity and honor, respect of self and respect of others, as the light and love that you are."

When they had finished, I noticed a symbol of four interconnected spirals glowing on my chest. Another gift, or a signifying mark? Perhaps I had been gifted this as a reminder of my initiation into the loving ways of spirit and in honor of successfully concluding this journey. I just wasn't sure of its meaning. This is my last memory of my journey to Amenti.

With a flash of light, I was again under my old friend the elm tree. The first thing I did was look down to my chest. The four spirals continued to quietly glow. I found a seven-strand copper-colored bracelet of light with sacred symbols on each wrist. I looked around and saw my guide near me.

My radiant friend smiled and said, "There are a

few more things you need to know. This symbol of four spirals represents each of the four fundamental aspects of love – Loving Wisdom, Loving Kindness, Loving Strength and Loving Being-ness. Notice how each spiral flows into another and yet they are one. Think of these as the four chambers of the heart. Once balanced within consciously and energetically, the heart can heal both physically and emotionally and express true love.

"Now, what is true love? Mary Magdalene says this: 'True love is of the heart and contains courage, strength and wisdom. True love is the all-encompassing energy of God's Grace and infinite blessings as expressed through the heart. Love is an infinite circle of energy that gives to receive and receives to give. Yet true love does not rely on this two-way energy exchange. It just is. It is an expression of goodness and grace that leads the way to joy.'

"Now, what is Joy? Joy is Love expressed. Joy is when love is released out into the world."

She paused to let this sink in.

"When we think, we create. When we feel, we create. And the energy of that creation becomes an aspect of us. Understand that from moment to moment our thoughts are creating our reality, and how we think and feel is profoundly affecting the resonance of our energy field. The vibration of our energy field, in turn, affects how we think and feel. If you deliberately practice the creation of these energies of the four fundamental aspects of love, these vibrations will, with repetition, become you. And you become them.

"The most important thing about the four fundamental aspects of love is the connection through practicing Loving Wisdom with the truth of the soul. Loving Wisdom – tuning in and hearing the voice of the heart – is the wellspring of loving creation. All else follows.

"If we look at each of the four aspects of love, we find the first aspect, Loving Wisdom, means being connected to the truth of your higher self. Once you accept this, you are on the pathway to happiness. It is the capacity to tune in to the soul's and heart's guidance to then find Loving Kindness within yourself, which always starts with loving compassion for yourself.

"Loving Kindness, the second aspect, is being kind to yourself first and then letting that kindness flow to others. This loving compassion honors your soul. Once we balance Loving Wisdom with Loving Kindness, we can then move into Loving Strength, the third aspect of love.

"Loving Strength is being true to yourself; of standing in the strength of your heart, applying these understandings to your life and taking the actions needed to follow the Loving Wisdom of the heart. It requires surrender, honor and courage. Surrender is letting go of what you cannot orchestrate or control in your life and trusting God and the universe to always guide you along the path of the heart. Surrender is not giving up; it is letting go and letting God. Honor is operating from integrity, honoring the rights of others as you would honor the rights of yourself. Courage is inner strength – determination – where all things and all dreams become possible.

"You need to release all aspects of control and follow your heart voice to stand in your heart strength, ensuring that love will find a way. Always honor yourself. It always takes courage to do what is right for yourself and not someone else.

"Practice the first three aspects to get to the point of Loving Being-ness, the fourth aspect of love. The goal is to be the love that leads you to being joy, balanced with giving and receiving love.

"My best advice now is to guard your mind from all low forms of thinking. Transform all doubt into radiant light. Know that forever your soul is now flying free as the butterfly flies in the light.

"Do not fight with your heart's voice, or higher self, when you feel peace and rightness. It always knows what is right for you. When we let go and surrender, we feel happy and at peace, no matter what is outwardly occurring in our lives. When we hold on to control we become stressed, anxious, irritable and depressed. Depression is just an indication that we are *not* listening to the voice of the heart or are too afraid to move forward and act on what the heart's voice, the loving wisdom of our soul, is guiding us to do.

"Know that you hold the strength. Know that within you lies the key to release. The key is the love you create in yourself. That key is the peace that you hold in your soul. That key is the thoughts that you send to your body. The image is deep in the mind that you hold.

"So stand in the light of the truth that you are. Within you is the image of God. Join together in oneness – in brotherly, sisterly love. Trust the eternal love and the universe to guide you always along the path of the heart.

Trust in God in your deepest desires. Your dreams reflect the truth of your soul.

"Last, I want you to feel within your heart for the authentic truth of yourself. Recognize the beautiful soul that you are and always have been. This is the time to reconnect with your authentic self and be the love that you are. Remember this."

Then, with a whisper of a breeze, she was gone.

I blinked away the suddenness of her leaving and was not sure of the passage of time, although the sun still shone as brightly as before. I passed through the round moon gate to go home. I glanced back and was astonished at the beauty it had become. The first twelve letters of the Hebrew alphabet now flamed gold around the circle. A veil of circles filled the opening, although I could still see the field and trees behind it. As much as I wanted to stare for hours, I felt a need to rest and settle my thoughts. One more glance back and I saw that it had vanished. The peace-filled field, the trees and the round gate were gone. Only a narrow path along a moss-covered wall through the woods remained to be seen.

Slowly walking home on a still glorious day, I counted my blessings in wonder and gratitude. I wasn't sure what exactly happened or if it had happened at all. I felt like I was in a trance. Perhaps I still am.

With the intention to help others, I have been guided to write the compositions attached to this story. May they provide gentle guidance in a loving voice. May the reader find their own answers and balance within.

I have gone back to Amenti a number of times, each

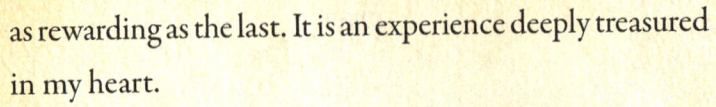

as rewarding as the last. It is an experience deeply treasured in my heart.

The memory of the four-spiral glyph serves as a reminder of my lessons. However, the mystery of the seven-strand copper-colored bracelets of light with sacred symbols that encircle my wrists still remains.

I have discovered a good number of things about myself. I learned how to live these concepts most of the time. I learned that I am a Guardian of Ascended Mother Earth, and a servant of the Trinity Lords and the Lords of Amenti. I am a friend of the Venusian Kamaras and Keeper of the Venusian Amethyst Flame on Gaia.

Most important, I learned that I live to serve the Light of the One. This is my joy, my honor, my purpose and my truth. And so I AM.

The Invitation

O, gentle child, with eyes of love,
how softly shines your light
throughout the world
with wisdom old and holy in its might.

O, gentle child, with eyes that see
the beauty of each one
of God's sweet creatures,
young and old, and precious to the One.

O, gentle child, with ears that hear
the calling of the One
and joins with those who sing
the songs that are forever sung.

O, gentle child, with heart that loves
each living, light filled one,
come dance with joy and gratitude
forever in the sun.

The Journey

Major Life Transitions

The twenty-two compositions of the Journey section reflect the journey of life from childhood to old age. The births, the major events, the turning points and the challenging situations that may be encountered are represented. They may reflect current physical, mental, emotional or spiritual conditions experienced.

The Journey

Zero: Beginnings

O, beautiful child, adventurous and bold,
Go to that place where you can show
The love in your heart, and all that you hold,
For all sweet life above and below.

For in the heart there is a light
And there you now must go
To live the love you've dreamed of
In visions long ago.

O, beautiful child, waste not now a moment,
As each one is precious and dear.
For the time has come to manifest and
To cast off all your fears.

Play in your dreams with courage and joy
The world is your magical toy.
Trust that God's Love will keep safe your next step
So go forward, go forward with the peace that you've kept!

*I am an innocent, free spirit, spontaneously
starting a new beginning.*

The Journey

One: Awareness

Awakened one, who swirls the ether,
And makes the world so bright.
Teach all how to conquer fear
And never take a fright.

For God always walks beside you
To wander in life streams
And smile with loving eyes on you
To manifest your dreams.

Use your power of concentration
To walk in loving light
And fill your chalice with sweet dreams
That last throughout the night.

O, Child of God, do you not hear
His gentle, loving call
That beckons you to come to him
And into his arms you fall?

I am a powerful person using skill, concentration and resourcefulness in my actions.

The Journey

Two: Intuition

O, sweet master, open the book
That holds the mysteries of life,
And partake the truth and all
That soothes all differences and strife.

For in the heart there lies within
A truth so deeply loved
And sent to you and, yes, to all.
The blessings from above.

Pay attention to your dreams
Where many clues are found.
Yet take your time to put in action
Those decisions not yet sound.

Sweet love of heart, know that you will
Trust the visions that you get
For in them lie your great reward
And peace without regret.

I am intuitive, mysterious, with higher powers.

The Journey
Three: Fertility

Beloved child, accept the gifts
Lavished from above,
Giving birth and nurturing your heart
In the One's eternal love.

For in abundance you will find
The golden light of grace
And share with all the wonders of
God's joy at love's own pace.

Vibrant work and creativity
Has earned its own reward.
Sprouting health, success and courage,
To flourish, going forward.

For the nature of your being,
In the One's nourishing light,
Is to be forever loving
And caring in this life.

I am beauty, fertility and abundance.

The Journey

Four: Authority

On solid foundation stands the One
To guide the hearts aloft
And manifest with gentleness
The structure of its love.

O, child of light, accept your choice
To be with brethren here,
To join with them, to lead the way,
Yet be forever near.

Cultivating logic
Creates a plan that's true.
Proceed with your convincing dreams
Inspiring others, too.

The light they see within your heart
Will surely show the way
And ever so they follow you
Every step along the way.

I am a solid foundation of structure and authority.

The Journey

Five: Tradition

O, sweet child, with eyes so wise
Enriched with fairness and faith,
Seek out the One, with heart so true
And in its love do bathe.

Alliances with those alike,
With those enjoined in love,
Can seek tradition and beliefs
To strengthen bonds of love.

Mentors, friends and family
Both here and far away
Can open up new support,
With morals and integrity.

Love and goodness enrich and help
The group in joyous delight
To help the search within each heart
For the meaning of their life.

I am guided by The One with my traditional values and beliefs.

The Journey

Six: Union

Beloved one, communicate
With those so near to you
The deep love that you hold for them
In your heart, forever true.

Stay close with those who share your love
Be it friend or family,
For in each heart there beats a joy
And thrill of harmony.

The union of shared values
Makes these choices seem so clear
Especially with those so close
And the ones you hold so dear.

So to the future you must look
To keep the vision bright
And hold in love the union sought
And well within the light.

I am love in all relationships, unions and choices.

The Journey

Seven: Victory

Sing, sweet child of victory!
For you successfully achieved
A personal sense of will power
Completing tasks that you conceived!

All can see the determined smile,
A sense of hard work done,
So raise a glass of gratitude
Celebrating with raucous fun.

The One approves and appreciates
The child who hears the call
And carries forth the victory
With fairness for one and all.

Within the corners of the heart
There is a light that shines,
And grounds you to beloved Earth
To continue for all time.

*I am in victorious control and determination as
I assert my will power.*

The Journey
Eight: Strength

Dear child, you stand so confident!
So straight and wise and true
That your decisions will reflect
The courage inside of you.

Your deeply grounded connections,
A heart infused with love,
Your eyes that see what's fair and just,
Guidance comes from up above.

With loving strength and heartfelt good,
You stand up for your beliefs,
And with compassion and control
You resist the injustice.

So make your choice! Take action now
With magnanimity!
And trust the One who guides us all
Into eternity.

I am strength, courage, control and compassion.

The Journey

Nine: Introspection

Beloved one, with quiet light
You hear the song of all,
The voice of inner guidance
And the music it enthralls.

That is how the wisdom comes,
So lovingly and soft
Yet filled with light and love and joy
Like breezes from aloft.

Seeking truth of your own heart
Is the path to be walked now.
Silently treading the light inside
To smooth your fretful brow.

Share the message as received.
Teach with love and grace
To lift the world into the light
That is its rightful place.

I am alone as I listen for inner guidance with introspection.

The Journey

Ten: Destiny

Lucky one, so full of hope,
So full of love divine,
That life will open all to you –
The best that it can find.

As the wheels of life turn round
Good luck and destiny
Will oversee your turning point.
Good fortune happens rapidly.

Grab the golden ring of life
The cycles turn your way
So gird your future with the light
The One will show the way.

Change occurs with benefits
Some hidden and some not.
But all come from the love of One
Enriching all you've got.

I am at a turning point of my life cycle with good luck, karma and destiny in play.

The Journey

Eleven: Justice

Dear one with a heart of gold
So full of gentle strength,
Be compassionate, kind and bold
For the heart's love is at stake.

Your spiritual core is full of love,
Learned on your mother's knee,
And wrapped in patience from above
With fairness and equity.

For with the cause and effect of life
There is only one best rule –
And that is to gently and fairly judge,
Preparing for renewal.

Truth and magic are the same
When gifted from the heart
To heal the wounded child with grace,
That sings out like a lark.

I am fairness and justice as truth exhibits the law of cause and effect.

The Journey
Twelve: Release

Sweet love, different views may help
To find a self you may not know
But be assured that in your heart
The light is sure to glow.

For the One is there to help release
All pain and heal the wound.
To rediscover the power within
A vibrancy renewed.

It is no sacrifice to release
Of that no longer needed
So let it go to a higher plane,
A selfless gift, love seeded.

Epiphanies and surprising gifts
May also come your way.
Review your plans, unique in love,
And claim a triumphant day.

I am releasing self-restrictions.

The Journey

Thirteen: Transition

Do not fear, my own sweet love,
Of beginnings, endings or change.
For in the swift transition lies
The transformation that's been arranged.

Release the old and accept the new
For the dawn of a new day nears
That the One has chosen just for you.
There is no need for tears.

Take your time, there is no rush.
Relief is sure to come.
Catch your breath and then proceed
With joyous music hum.

Adjust, move on and celebrate!
A new you to be grown.
And so we see the ecstasy of
The One's most glorious glow.

I am transforming as I move from beginning to end and back again.

The Journey

Fourteen: Balance

Dear one, balance your heart in light,
In gentle moderation,
Bringing to you the meaning of
Purposeful cooperation.

Compromise may rectify
Impulses made in haste.
Start with patience and forgiveness
Resulting in more grace.

With compassion and with kindness
Approach the other side
To reach a fruitful conversation
That blends the two divides.

For in the One there cannot be
A parting that does not heal.
For we are one and in that stand
Our futures have been sealed.

I am in balance as I moderate my purpose and meaning with patience.

The Journey
Fifteen: Redemption

My child, change focus and with haste!
Remember the love that is here.
The love that binds and bonds
All life and holds you oh so dear.

Do you see the walls you've built
Are false and filled with fear?
Binding, bonding to nothingness,
Escape is never near.

Entrapment in illusion
Is only in your mind.
Refusing to see the hands of love
Enjoining their hands with thine.

The One will ever be the peace
To fill the void you've built.
Redemption is for those who seek
Freedom from sadness and guilt.

I am breaking free and reclaiming my power.

The Journey

Sixteen: Upheaval

Sweet love, sudden change is now!
Take action that is needed!
You have ignored the warning signs
And they have gone unheeded.

You suddenly see the truth of all
And time is running out.
And liberation from illusion
Is due without a doubt.

Upheaval is on the way but yet
Revelation is now, too.
Awaken to the world of growth
To make the changes true.

Spread your wings and now take flight,
Disaster and fear behind you,
And live your purpose for the light
Liberation and love will guide you.

*I am acknowledging revelation through disaster,
upheaval and sudden change.*

The Journey

Seventeen: Renewal

Wishful child, eyes on the prize
With hope and serenity,
The path is chosen with the thought
Of renewal and spirituality.

Walk in light, in joy and love.
The angels guide the way
And soon you'll find your dreams
Fulfilled, with more to come today.

The future is bright, the burdens lost,
The path not so very long
And with excitement comes the fact
That your faith is always strong.

Celebrate when dreams come true,
When heartfelt song breaks out.
The world rejoices with each note
And cheers you on throughout.

I am serene and hopeful, with renewed spirituality.

The Journey

Eighteen: Illusion

Illusions and veils may hide the light
But do not fear, my love.
For your insights and your gifts
Will beam beyond the clouds.

The truth shines out from your heart
Dispersing all the dross
And in its place, a wonder,
Filled with hope, not a drop of loss.

For the One glows gently with the love
That only it can give
And illuminates the fearful heart
So you and all may live.

Be not afraid, do not despair.
Illusions are not true.
The One gives light to all who love
And revels in all who do.

I am no longer afraid of my illusions.

The Journey

Nineteen: Success

Blessed child, so full of love,
This time is just for you!
Sweet success and joyous fun
Are here the whole way through.

Vibrant health is yours and still
More warmth and confidence
Will surely come your way to stay
Starting from this moment hence.

Vitality will rule the day,
Each moment filled with light.
Great ideas and solutions will
Bring changes that delight!

Keeping life so positive
Will smoothly pave your path
To unexpected blessings
Across all horizons vast.

I am fun, warm, positive and successful.

The Journey
Twenty: Rebirth

You're on the threshold of major change.
This is surely true.
Your inner voice begs for release
And a direction entirely new.

Time to review and evaluate
Some old decisions made
And start the rebirth of your life.
New roads are to be laid.

Ask the One for guidance now.
It surely will be given.
Follow the light that shines ahead
Each precious step enlivened.

As the One will always forgive,
Every heart is held so dear.
Rejoice and sing with all the throng,
Celebrate with joyful cheers.

I am following my inner calling for a new life.

The Journey
Twenty-One: Integration

O, dear love, your work complete,
To new levels you arise
So celebrate and contemplate
Where your new contentment lies.

Integrate what you have learned,
The details that you know,
For in the joy of accomplishment
Are the seeds of horizons sown.

New perspectives fill your world,
Clear miracles on the rise,
Will surely slip into your life
To balance and peace devise.

All the children of this world
Come in with grace and love
Watched over and protected
With the love of those above.

I am integrated, completed and accomplished.

Loving Wisdom

Mental, Intellect, Air Element

Loving Wisdom is being connected to the truth of your soul, your higher self. Once you accept this, you are on the pathway to happiness. It is the capacity to tune in to the soul's and the heart's guidance. This is the section of the intellect where we make decisions in life and express our thoughts.

Loving Wisdom

One: Clarity

O, you quick magical one,
New ideas take flight!
Inspiration comes to you
Your plans are in the right.

Challenges do not block
But test your strength anew.
Making sure your every step
Is what you want to do.

Clarity disperses clouds
That have been circling you.
Confidence exalts your stance,
Your brilliance now shines through.

You see the truth before you now,
Replacing misconception.
Moving forward with new strength
And the power of inspiration.

I am clearly inspired by my visions.

THE FOUR FUNDAMENTAL ASPECTS OF LOVE

Loving Wisdom

Two: Indecision

O, dear one, you struggle so
Between two choices dear.
Decide which one will fill your heart
Then take action without fear.

Indecision holds you back
And makes life challenging.
So make a plan to carry forth
A new self-balancing.

Compromise may help you now
A wiggle here or two.
A little here, a little there but
Choose what's best for you

Avoidance will no longer work.
Push impasse aside.
Choose a brighter circumstance
And like the wind you'll ride.

I am choosing a new, well-balanced path.

Loving Wisdom

Three: Separation

O, my sweet heartbroken one,
Forgive what's in the past.
Use your heartfelt courage for
A new future to be cast.

Lean on others who may give
All the support you need,
Then turn around and share that love
With others who are in need.

Reaching out will heal the pain
With comfort and with love.
Opening your heart releases
Goodness from above.

It is natural for you to feel
Deep injury and loss.
Remember to forgive yourself
For missteps that have cost.

I am releasing the pain of loss.

THE FOUR FUNDAMENTAL ASPECTS OF LOVE

Loving Wisdom

Four: Recuperation

O, my love, you need to stop.
You need to meditate.
Give yourself a rest for now
From matters that escalate.

Set aside all concerns
To rest and rejuvenate
For the body and the mind
Need to recuperate.

Clarity of mind
Results from this retreat.
Reflection on these matters
Provides answers that you seek.

The world will go on spinning
But your world needs to pause.
Exhaustion needs to be expunged
To contemplate what was.

I am resting, recuperating and contemplating.

Loving Wisdom

Five: Betrayal

O, my child, troubles have come
(And paid at your expense)
From a person with no integrity
And with no good intent.

What you thought was a good choice
Turns out to be not so
And not worth all your effort
Or regret-filled tears of woe.

So walk away with head held high
And gratitude flowing out
For you have learned your lesson now.
Relieved of all your doubts.

A brighter path still lies ahead.
Your kindness to be returned.
Light from the One will show the way
To the happiness that you've earned.

I am courageous and strong after betrayal.

Loving Wisdom
Six: Passage

O, sweet dear, please look ahead
And do not look behind you.
The worst has past and now you meet
A future that defines you.

Winds of change are blowing now
With promise of good times.
Sunnier horizons and
Happier shores will now be thine.

Burdens have been lifted.
Relief has now arrived.
Raising eyes in gratitude,
Your joy has been revived.

Horizon bright with joy and love.
Sweet passage of new life.
Embrace new dawns and with the One
Your future now is ripe.

*I am grateful for this necessary transition
as a rite of passage.*

Loving Wisdom

Seven: Deception

O, my dear, are you deceived
Or are you the deceiver?
Stealthy words belie the truth
To the most trusting believer.

Review your plans to make sure.
Disappointments become clear.
Time passes by and provides
Better choices for you here.

Truth in action and in word
Demands in caution be.
For overlooked omissions
May prove sad destiny.

Ask the One to show you who
Integrity prevails.
Listen closely to your heart
So your endeavors do not fail.

I am choosing honesty and honor.

Loving Wisdom

Eight: Imprisonment

O, my sweet deluded one,
Do you not see the trap
That you have made yourself
That has just one small gap?

Use that gap and leap out
Of the prison that you made.
It's all within your mind
And memories will soon fade.

You have the power of what it takes
To free yourself within,
To dance with the joy and laughter
That life has gladly given.

Self-belief and commitment
Will come in handy now.
As the One smiles down on you
To strengthen your resolve.

I am freeing myself from self-imposed isolation.

Loving Wisdom

Nine: Depression

O, worried one, who cannot sleep,
Tossed with nightmares so.
Fear has replaced your peace.
Despair is sure to show.

Breathing deep and slowly
Helps push the stress away.
Walk in woods or on the beach
To keep your stress at bay.

Regrets are not worth your time.
Obsession on them, too,
Will steal the joy of your day
And all the evening through.

Writing down your thoughts
To give your angels dear
Softens up your tensions
And rids you of your fears.

I am focused on calm thoughts and hope.

Loving Wisdom

Ten: Defeat

O, wounded one, it's time to leave.
To journey on in life.
For there is nothing left for you
In this place of strife.

This notes a beginning.
An embrace of future joy.
This ends a painful period
And a recovery to employ.

Sometimes endings can be sad,
Others in relief,
Choose the one that you prefer
And start to move your feet!

A new horizon opens up and
Is ripe with happiness
And lifts the burdens of the past.
You have earned your bliss!

I am not defeated by betrayal, loss and endings.

Loving Wisdom

Eleven: Curious

O, curious one, a challenge lay
Between you and another one.
Be honest and be frank.
Be forthright and be done.

You can tell a lie
Between the lines of talk.
You can see another lie
By the way they walk.

Please tell the truth with kindness
Be mindful of your tongue.
A heart is easily broken
Before your speech is done.

Let your spiel be positive.
Inform and then uplift.
Honesty can be a curse
But also a sweet gift.

I am energetic, curious, talkative and mentally alive.

Loving Wisdom

Twelve: Opinionated

O, high-speed racer, acting fast
And thinking faster now.
Going like the wind
That blows behind your prow.

An unstoppable go-getter!
Destination undefined.
Take time to see your options
Before off the cliff you dive.

Flashing bright like lightning
Brings unexpected change.
Thrilling with the tide of action
Not noticing the range.

Take a moment now to see
The cost of speed to those
Whom you have left behind to be
A witness to your mood.

I am valuing my opinion as well as others'.

Loving Wisdom

Thirteen: Perceptive

O, perceptive child of light,
So organized and quick,
Your independence of thought
Will show the world your wit.

Separating wheat from chaff,
Based on experience,
Frees your life to focus on
The path before you hence.

Taking life with grain of salt,
And a little grin as well,
Prepares you for the road ahead
With humor that will tell.

Strong and with prosperity,
Your life defined by you,
Self-sufficient in your ways
Evident in all you do.

I am an organized, perceptive, independent quick thinker.

Loving Wisdom

Fourteen: Intellectual

O, balanced one, you hold a scale
To judge the fairness of
A situation that's in need
Of an answer based in love.

Impartial and fair-minded,
Experienced and a pro,
Your advice is now needed
To decide a confusing row.

Romance may not suit you.
Your field of choice preferred
To candlelight and cuddling.
That choice is deferred.

The One still shines within you
And depends on all your skills.
For clarity of thought
Will equalize the dueling wills.

I am a clear thinking, confident, intellectual power for the truth.

Loving Kindness

Emotions, Relationships, Water Element

Loving Kindness is being kind to yourself first and then letting that kindness flow to others. This loving compassion honors your soul. This section concerns emotions and relationships that may bring spiritual growth.

Loving Kindness

One: Love

O, dear child, love flows to you,
Opening hearts and eyes.
Refreshing or to make anew
For that is the way of the wise.

Rivers of joy come rushing your way
With waterfalls of love
Faith renewed abundantly
And joy gleaned from above.

Hearts in love shown to be soft,
And eyes that shine so bright.
Conversations that exhilarate
And last throughout the night.

Falling in love is so divine
So very human, too,
Each day's burdens are lightened now
To dance the whole day through.

I am love, compassion and creativity.

Loving Kindness

Two: Relationships

O, beautiful child, how wonderful
To fall in love so deep!
To unite in partnership,
In a union that will keep.

Two becoming one in heart,
To love and be loved true,
Is a dream of every child.
A blending through and through.

But if the two are in dispute,
Accusations deemed unfair,
Resolve to reconcile
With forgiveness in the air.

Sharing life together is
A challenge day by day.
But guided by a love that's shared
Will surely pave the way.

I am united in partnership and love.

Loving Kindness

Three: Celebration

O, my dear, let's celebrate!
A party is now due
With joyful news and good fortune
Complete with gratitude.

The One will play the music.
Dancing as you may!
Friends will come from all around
To share with you this day.

Embracing in this moment
All the blessings from above.
Laughter, smiles and hugs abound,
The graces of sweet love.

You hold the spark of God inside.
You're a blessed being here.
So gladly shine your light around
To ignite a higher tier.

I am celebrating friendship and community.

Loving Kindness

Four: Contemplation

O, dear love, it went so fast!
An opportunity missed!
It stood right in front of you!
If it were a snake, it'd hiss.

As you are distracted
And you cannot see,
The forest grows around you
But you can't see it for the trees.

Go out into Nature.
She is waiting there for you
To help calm and quiet your mind
And maybe a prayer or two.

Reevaluate your stand
The solution is here, too.
Open your eyes to the world
And those who would help you.

I am envisioning new opportunities.

Loving Kindness

Five: Despair

O, my love, please look away
To the silver lining here.
For spilled milk is not to drink.
There is more that is near.

Refocus on your peace within.
The One shines brightly there.
The future has so much for you
But not if you despair.

Mourning loss needs be short-lived.
Bereavement has its place.
Not in your future but the past.
Not ever as your base.

There are those who will help.
Recovery is their goal.
Recovering a future bright,
Forgiveness makes you whole.

I am accepting loss but moving forward.

Loving Kindness

Six: *Nostalgia*

O, my sweet, enchanted child,
The world rebounds in joy
In your dreams and memories.
Nostalgic in their ploys.

Remember how you'd play and dance
And twirl inside the wind?
To have the sun upon your face
And contentedness within?

Retrieve the brightness of those days,
So magical and inspired.
Rekindle the innocence of the love
You need now and desire.

Infuse your life with that great light,
So deep and pure and stable,
To benefit you at this time
And do the best you're able.

I am nostalgic with innocent memories.

Loving Kindness

Seven: Choices

O, wish-filled one, the time has come
To make decisions true.
Focus and get busy!
No more delay for you!

Daydreaming has its use
To make the options clear
But you have used that time up!
Choose wisely and start here.

Make a plan with your choice.
Putting actions to each step.
Then follow through with stronger voice
To fill each one with pep.

The One will guide you on your way
Spread your wings for heaven bound
But do not fly too close to the sun
Nor stay upon the ground.

I am filled with imagination and wishful thinking.

Loving Kindness

Eight: Disappointment

O, dear one, now is the time
You've chosen to move on
To greater things in life or love.
Now comes a beautiful dawn.

A new day starts to shine on you.
A new way to begin.
A new path towards happiness.
A new goodness from within.

This turning point has come with love
To show the way towards truth.
Shedding the past in grateful ways
That show your light is true.

Deeper into your heart you go
To search for meaning and gifts
And show the world a brand new you,
Bright with a love that lifts.

I am pleased with my new positive direction.

Loving Kindness

Nine: Satisfaction

O, dear love, a moment great!
Your wishes have come true!
Your dreams are now fulfilled at last
With magic and renewal!

The One has heard your heartfelt prayers
And lovingly pronounced
That today they will come true
And sorrow will be trounced!

Celebrate with awe and wonder
Celebrate with play and song
Celebrate the One's light within
That shines away the wrongs.

Pleasures will abound for now
A joy now manifests
To fill your face with crinkly smiles
And well-placed happiness.

I am happy and satisfied for my wishes are fulfilled.

Loving Kindness

Ten: Harmony

O, contented one, rejoice!
The rainbow glows 'round you!
The balanced life that you live
Rewards with family true!

Trusted friends or bloodline,
The best that life affords,
Makes a life worth living
Sung in euphoric chords.

Make a space every day
For those you love to love.
Watch them grow under your care
And loving eyes above.

Your life is truly heaven sent!
The One will glow about
The wonder that is you, my love,
And it cannot do without.

I am happy that there is harmony in my relationships.

Loving Kindness

Eleven: Synchronicity

O, young one, here comes a love
To tempt your heart anew.
To sing your praises with aplomb
And tempt you with renewal.

Will you give your heart so free
And with abandonment?
Will you soar in sweet embrace
Without embarrassment?

As the One can see your joy
With sparkling laughter flowing,
Eyes filled with light that shines around
And radiates in knowing.

Love is yours this joy-filled day
Each moment encased with light.
Golden moments that will stay
Touched with sheer delight.

I am a creative messenger for new beginnings and synchronicity.

Loving Kindness

Twelve: Charm

O, you flirt! You dreamy one!
Your heart so full of love!
Then you hastily change your mind
And leave a heart-broke one.

You can focus on one heart
Until your eye may wander
Then off to the races you will run
To find the love of another.

Uninterested in consequence,
A trail of sorrow and woe
Follow behind you in a wake
Of the broken hearts you've sown.

Balance your need for newness
Or emptiness of life
Will surely be your future
In loneliness and strife.

I am imagining romance and charm.

Loving Kindness
Thirteen: Calm

O, my dear and reliable friend!
How calm you are with news
To help the others stand
With truth. You never do refuse.

Be mindful of giving away too much
(Your heart will not agree)
But you need care as well, my dear,
Make time now to receive.

Bolster your serenity
With self-love and tenderness
Strengthening your reserves
By refueling your loving zest.

The One can see your every grace,
Your love that so abounds,
And sends you all the light you need
For you to spread around.

I am calm, intuitive and compassionate.

THE FOUR FUNDAMENTAL ASPECTS OF LOVE

Loving Kindness

Fourteen: Counselor

O, sweet counselor, listen well
And speak now from your heart.
Those comforted by your words
Hold you as trusted and smart.

The care with which your every sound
Will heal the wounds so deep
And lighten up the world around
And into dreams they leap.

With honor and integrity,
Kind words protect the peace.
Leading others far beyond
And into the truth they seek.

With clarity of thought
And wise, judicious ways
You mediate with compassion
That shines throughout your days.

I am balanced and in control.

Loving Strength

Passions, Action, Fire Element

Loving Strength is being true to yourself, standing in the strength of your heart, applying these understandings to your life and taking the actions needed. It requires surrender, courage and integrity. This section is about taking action, especially with passion and creativity, showing enthusiasm and conviction.

Loving Strength

One: Potential

O, my love, a fresh start!
A new adventure now awaits.
Begin with power and inspire
With action from the gate.

New potential and ideas
Rise up with joy and strength
To help you learn in mastery
And go the journey's length.

Create the world you want to see.
Forgive with loving heart
Finding comrades that you seek
And rarely be apart.

This new beginning is filled with joy.
A start of a new life.
Trust your vision and create,
And be loving with insight.

I am inspired as I create a new beginning.

Loving Strength

Two: Discovery

O, sweet one, with future bright,
Courageous choices made
To come onto your path alone
Or as companions bade.

A wonder-filled world is all about
To shape as you know how.
Share with those whose dreams,
Like yours, will rocket to the stars.

With steady progress, step by step,
Each moment you will see
The joy of love and companionship
That rewards complicity.

The love of friends who share your path,
Taking chances along with you,
Spurs the love that will urge you on
Succeeding as only few do.

I am planning a new future with good decisions.

Loving Strength

Three: Expansion

O, dear one, look forward now.
Your next step to be taken
And plan ahead for the success
That in your light awakens.

You've long prepared for this day
With insight and with love
To travel the full journey
With the help shone from above.

The One increases your gifts today
Be sure of that, my dear,
And satisfaction is yours to stay
As its light is always here.

Patience wills your dreams to bloom
Each and every day
Hard work has accomplished much
And prepares you for the way.

I am moving forward with foresight, enterprise and preparation.

Loving Strength

Four: Homecoming

O, my child, it's time to rest,
For reining in your peace.
Go back home in riches.
The fighting now will cease.

Harmony is your reward
Of hard-fought battle won.
So celebrate with others who
Can see what has been done.

Blessings in the community
And within the home
Are counted in the millions,
Securing all that comes.

Manifest in gratitude,
Dance with pride and joy
For blessings flow in circles
With each prayer that's employed.

*I am supported and secure at home and
in my community.*

Loving Strength

Five: Conflict

O, my love, be ever clear!
Keep focus to the end.
Little things surround you now
That challenge your intent.

Gadflies buzz, distract and bother
But you need to see your way
Through to completion with success
And not your mind to stray.

Opposing goals, different opinions
Are at odds with what's held dear.
Keep solutions at the top,
Not the drama wrapped in fear.

The One shines bright a column
To lead you on in light
And keep you feeling optimistic
Unhindered by the fight.

I am respectful of others' ideas and learn from them.

Loving Strength

Six: Confidence

O, my sweet, victorious one!
Great news is on the way!
The people recognize good deeds
And follow in your sway.

Bravo! Sweet success is thine
And seen beyond your sight.
Others celebrate with you
To bask within your light.

Do not be humble or be shy.
Good fortune smiles on you.
With glowing confidence you show
The artistry you do.

This day shows the love of all
Held deep within your heart
Then spread to others with great cheer,
Joining hands and hearts.

I am proud of my success.

Loving Strength

Seven: Perseverance

O, brave one, stand your ground!
Never to back down!
For you are in the right
And they are in the wrong.

Choose your battles wisely,
Defending your beliefs,
Persevere with love and hope
Then on to victory.

There may be others who envy
Your strength in adversity.
So stay alert and vigilant
To ward off their jealousy.

The One will surely protect your win
And smiles upon the grace
That you show your adversaries
And shimmers from your face.

I am determined to reach my goals.

Loving Strength

Eight: Acceleration

O, sweet love, this is the pace
Of an arrow in the wind,
And puts into action what's desired
And makes your head to spin.

Now is the time. Now is the place.
No delay can ever be.
For now the change will come
Accelerated with priority.

This is not the time to fear.
So many things at once.
Hold on tight and manifest
The dreams of what you want.

Hope will help your grounding for
Frenzied action will abound
And take you to your awaited end
To thrill in grace and sound!

I am bursting with energy and ideas.

Loving Strength

Nine: Persistence

O, courageous eagle,
So persistent in your faith,
This is a test of resilience
To the opposition faced.

Defend and protect the work
Of hard-earned gains you've made
For this will surely urge you on
To the finish without fade.

Your ability to believe in love
Will strengthen your resolve.
Your wisdom and your stamina
Bring a situation to a close.

Listening with open heart
To others who disagree
Helps to close the gap
And make new friends more easily.

I am persistent and never give up.

THE FOUR FUNDAMENTAL ASPECTS OF LOVE

Loving Strength
Ten: Responsibility

O, sweet one, whose burdens weigh
The world on your shoulders deep.
Put down your load, get some rest,
Your worries will surely keep.

Balance is the key for now
To achieve a healthy glow.
Hard work and stress have come and
Thrown off your balance and flow.

You need play to lighten up!
To let the child within
Smile and laugh with family
To turn down all the din.

The gains you've made will still be here
Protected by the One.
The love you hold will guide you through,
Forever loved, then done.

I am delegating responsibilities so I may rest.

Loving Strength

Eleven: Enthusiasm

O, free spirit, with your love
Of exploration do
Rely on the light of the One
That beams inside of you.

With enthusiasm you
Go forward and with haste
To capture the thrills of discovery.
Not a moment do you waste.

Challenges arise and yet
Your ingenuity defeats
All the obstacles that impede.
Their ending is complete.

Go forth into horizons
With speed and confidence
The One enfolds you in love
And walks beside you hence!

I am a free spirit embracing discovery and exploration.

Loving Strength

Twelve: Impulsiveness

O, beloved, this is it.
Your restlessness confirmed.
For, suddenly, the time is here
To use the lessons learned.

Impulses use more energy.
But darling, be aware:
Think things through more carefully
So action can be fair.

Adventure is exciting
And passion is so, too
But the future is so fraught
With what has to do with you.

Protect your loved ones and preserve
The love surrounding you
By avoiding rash decisions
When recklessness ensues.

I am vibrant with clear visions and calculated risks.

Loving Strength

Thirteen: Vibrancy

O, dear love, you warm the hearts
Of those who look to you
For leadership and gentle thoughts,
Determination, too.

Spread your wings, you know the way.
Be ever confident.
Those who follow will support
Independent exuberance.

They see you as the leader who
Will shine on ever bright
And reignite them when in need
Whenever they lose sight.

Vibrant love will fill the gaps
When you forget your grace.
Forgiving in the moment when
Your love may slip from haste.

I am exuberant, warm, bold and determined.

Loving Strength

Fourteen: Vision

O, dear love, with vision strong
Lead others to the One in song.
For in your honor and your heart
Lies the way that makes your mark.

Lion strong with charm and flair,
Achieve what others never dare.
Uniting others of every hue
With your ideals shining through.

Activate your throngs with light.
Motivate them with delight.
For you possess the true beliefs
That see you through without relief.

The One shines on you now to show
The path for others so they may know
How to make a change in life
And love one another without strife.

I am a natural-born leader with vision and honor.

Loving Being-ness

Material, Physical, Earth Element

Loving Being-ness is being joyful from a place of peace, being the love that leads to being joy with the balance of giving and receiving love. It means to be joyful in walking the path of the new way while connected to the soul's guidance. Trust that you will be shown the way. This section is about the material world that includes the body, health, home, security and finances.

Loving Being-ness

One: Prosperity

O, smiling one, you surely know
Abundance is here now.
Manifesting all your dreams
Of prosperity and love.

You faithfully kept the light within
And nurtured all with bliss.
Now you reap the benefits
Enhancing your happiness.

Unexpected gifts come now
To elevate your life
With new opportunities
Of plans with deep insight.

Feeling blessed with high hopes
Entranced in dreams abound,
You now seek to infuse with joy
All beings that surround.

*I am manifesting new financial opportunity
and prosperity.*

Loving Being-ness
Two: *Adaptability*

O, child of joy, be playful
In all the work you do
Balancing the drudge with
Little laughs and sly smiles, too.

Adapting to the many demands
Exhausts the strongest soul.
But humor lightens every load
And speedily the time will go.

Prioritize the tasks assigned
Appropriately to the scene.
Share the fun and the sludge
With others on the team.

The One is here to help you through
With anything that you need.
Lifting hearts in oneness
To complete all of your deeds.

*I am balanced, adaptable and prioritize
my time-management.*

Loving Being-ness

Three: Collaboration

O, good child, hold our hand
To go to work and learn
How to live a life of love and
Not to bridges burn.

Others hold the key to life
Of growing confidence
In love and companionship
To use all of your talents.

Creating teams of friends
Who share your passions dear
Ensures sweet success in life
Along a path that's clear.

Love of work can be a beacon
For those who seek the same.
Fulfillment in a job well done
When all your fears are tamed.

I am embracing teamwork and collaboration.

Loving Being-ness

Four: Stability

O, precious love, please be aware
Of those around you who
Take advantage of your sweetness
To confuse the facts for you.

Good decisions are readily made
With head and heart aligned.
Controlling your security
With hints from the Divine.

Resources wisely managed
And the gifts of charity
Stabilize all your worth
To live abundantly.

Giving to less fortunate
Circles around to you.
For this is the way of life.
This is the Golden Rule.

I am managing my finances wisely.

Loving Being-ness

Five: Isolation

O, my love, do not worry!
Ask and you'll receive,
For the One hears your cries
Of lack and poverty.

Your loss is not as deep as fear
Would have you to believe
For it is in its nature
To lie and to deceive.

You are not alone in this.
Angels are standing by
To change your matters for the good
And all your tears to dry.

So say your prayers with good intent
Reversing all your pain
And look for the help that is here
To make you whole again.

I am grateful for all of my present and future blessings.

Loving Being-ness

Six: Generosity

O, dear love, tell me now,
Are you the giver or the receiver?
Abundance is on the way to those
Who are the true believers.

Believe with all your heart
In the love that flows to you.
Believe with all your heart
That it is sweet and deep and true.

From that love you provide
The fertile ground within
That the harvest multiplies
As to others it is given.

The One loves a grateful heart
Rewarding with more gifts
And balancing the treasure with
A joy that truly lifts.

I am thankful to be so blessed that I can share my wealth with charity.

Loving Being-ness

Seven: Reward

O, my child, be patient please.
Wait for the seed to grow.
The harvest is so very near
As your field of dreams now shows.

Deep-rooted dreams within your heart
Spur your vision forward.
Paving roads with your hard work
To a future that's rewarded.

Your fruits of labor ever grow
To be picked when they are ready.
Pausing now to plan next steps
To keep your profits steady.

Treasure comes now to fruition
A testament to your love
Profiting your world with hope
And gifts from up above.

I am assured my sustained investments will return tangible rewards.

Loving Being-ness
Eight: Education

O, adored student of life,
It's time to learn new skills
Or hone the ones that you have
To give your heart new thrills.

Seminars or classes
Apprenticeships or the like
Will lift your spirits with the hope
Of improving your lot in life.

A quality education
Can come in many forms.
Engaging you with new crafts
To raise you from the norms.

Choose wisely after research
For on this path you'll stay
Showing that you're living
In a brighter way.

I am dedicated to improving my situation through constant learning and growth.

Loving Being-ness
Nine: Discipline

O, you self-reliant one,
Hard work and dedication
Have brought you to a place of peace
And moments of reflection.

Achieving much demands a rest.
A pause righteously earned
Restoring peace within your heart
And happiness returned.

Just this little luxury
Of spending time alone
Buys a lot of incentive
To continue carrying on.

The One can see your weariness
And blesses you once more
To carry out the work of light
With blessings held in store.

I am grateful for the fruits of my labors.

Loving Being-ness
Ten: Accomplishment

O, dear heart, do you see
Completion is at hand?
For you have worked and saved
For all your future plans.

Security is quite assured.
Bringing freedom from your worries.
Retire in good faith that all
Your fears have now been buried.

Focus on the family with
Confidence that all is well.
Honoring your heritage
By histories you will tell.

Caring warmth binds the love
To hold the family close,
Drawing comfort from each other
Blessing each with loving dose.

I am proud of my accomplishments.

Loving Being-ness

Eleven: Manifestation

O, happy optimistic one,
Knowledge is a must
To learn how to make your way
Through a world you dare not trust.

Make a plan to carry through
A dream you've held awhile
Then follow it to manifest
Sweet success with profit piled.

Frugalness and patience long
Is needed for your pocket.
Supporting future endeavors with
Each line item on your docket.

Good news about your clever plans,
Abundance from the One
Nudges you into the light
With dreams bright as a sun!

I am able to manifest my visions and goals.

Loving Being-ness
Twelve: Methodical

O, guardian angel child of mine,
So deep in cautious plans
Take action now for it is time
To proudly make a stand.

Courageous ways will surely show
Your care and dedication
To every detail that allows
Pure joy and pure elation.

What may seem routine to you
Others may see as divine.
What may seem everyday to you
Others may see as very kind.

Goodness of heart always implies
A closeness with the One
That overcomes each obstacle
And a loving kindness done.

I am committed to my path of successful completion.

Loving Being-ness
Thirteen: Practical

O, my warm and caring child,
So quick to lend a hand,
Helping others less fortunate
In air or sea or on land.

Magic swirls around you now.
"Form and Function" is your goal.
Prosperity affords the choices made
Yet discernment has its role.

Loving family and friends
Comes naturally to you.
Swooping in to save the day
And making dreams come true.

Creating beauty in the world
With what is present here
Is your gift from the One
Who loves you, oh, so dear!

I am resourceful, with down-to-earth solutions.

Loving Being-ness

Fourteen: Abundance

O, my sweet, compassionate one,
The one with heart of gold.
Your love now returns to you
With rewards of treasure told.

Your "Midas Touch" has traveled now
From work into your heart.
Helping others in this world,
Your riches to impart.

You are bound to save this world,
Your little corner in it,
Rejoicing throngs appreciate
Your efforts to help win it.

Enjoy the fruits of life today
Smile and laugh with glee
For the One is on your side
And forever it shall be.

I am successful at attracting and managing abundance.

About This Book

Topics mentioned in the story are:
- In "The Story," after we pass through each gate, we bow to the light of the guardians. "The light" here refers to the Light of God within each being's heart. The bow serves as a gesture of gratitude and respect for them and for the God within.
- The Trinity Lords, consisting of Lord Michael, Lord Metatron and Lord Melchizedek.
- The Lords of Amenti – a group of seven magnificent beings who oversee the Earth. They reside within a pocket of frequency where all timelines, sequences and harmonics relating to the Earth intersect. The Lords are related to our seven chakras – 3, 4, 5 and 6, 7, 8 and 9.
    o Root chakra – 3: Untanas, Lord of death and hidden magic, all things mortal, the underworld
    o Sacral chakra – 4: Quertas, Lord of life, loosens power, frees souls

- o   Solar plexus chakra – 5: Chietal, Lord of magic and Master of all
- o   Heart chakra – 6: Goyana, Lord of light
- o   Throat chakra – 7: Huertal, Lord of space and time, chakra of imagination, imagination being free from all space and time
- o   Third eye chakra – 8: Semveta, Weigher of human hearts, speeding up and slowing progression
- o   Crown chakra – 9: Ardal, Lord of lords, holder of the white light; crown chakra is the divine
- The transformed stone moon gate is pure fiction that blends the sacred geometry symbol of the flower of life with the Jewish esoteric symbol of the Sepher Yetzirah. The origins of both are too ancient to be available to historians, although my research into both seems to point to originally similar meanings overall.
- The Venusian Kumaras are associated with Ascended Master Sanat Kumara, who is the Father of the Brotherhood and Sisterhood of White Light on Earth. He is the Flame Holder of the Violet Flame of Freedom of God for Earth.

About the Author

Cheryl Jackson grew up on the St. Clair River in Michigan. She attained a Bachelor's Degree in Communication Graphics from the University of Michigan, Ann Arbor, where she met her husband. She moved to Raleigh, North Carolina, with her husband, and continues to reside there with their dogs.

Cheryl has been a student of metaphysical concepts for over 30 years. Much of the basis of her knowledge came from Diana Henderson, a local angel and ascended master communicator. She added the teachings of Judy Satori in 2015 and continues to study Judy's teachings, which include sound healing as well as angel, ascended master, and multigalactic communication. Cheryl was granted permission by Judy Satori and Spirit to continue the teachings of Mary Magdalene.

Acknowledgments

I acknowledge that without the support and patience of my friends Carmen Moa Rivera, Karen Webb Gwyn, Diana Henderson, Marcia McCollum Hebrank, Judy Satori and my fabulous husband and dogs, this book would not have been possible.

The professional expertise of Christine Kloser, Carrie Jareed, and the folks at Capucia Publishing made the process as smooth and painless as a book could ever be. They are superb and outstanding as people and professionals.

May my everlasting gratitude and multitudes of blessings bring them tsunamis of joy and bliss.

Thank you seems so inadequate, but it's all I have left.

Thank you,
Cheryl Jackson
Guardian of Ascended Mother Earth, servant of the Trinity Lords and the Lords of Amenti, friend of the Venusian Kamaras and Keeper of the Venusian Amethyst Flame on Gaia.

I live to serve the Light of the One. This is my joy, my honor, my purpose, and my truth. And so I AM.